D1505092

A Gift For:

_____

From:

_____

Thank You
for Being You

BRADLEY TREVOR GREIVE

Andrews McMeel
Publishing, LLC

Thank You for Being You copyright © 2008 by BTG Studios Pty Ltd. All rights reserved. No part of this book may be used or reproduced in any manner whatsoever without written permission except in the case of reprints in the context of reviews. For information, write Andrews McMeel Publishing, LLC, an Andrews McMeel Universal company, 4520 Main Street, Kansas City, Missouri 64111.

This edition published in 2013 by Hallmark Gift Books LLC, a division of Hallmark Cards, Inc.

Visit us on the Web at Hallmark.com

ISBN: 978-1-59530-597-8
BOK1248

Printed and bound in China

Thank You
for Being You

PHOTO CREDITS

NIGEL DENNIS / AFRICA IMAGERY • www.africaimagery.com
JEAN-MICHEL LABAT / AUSCAPE • www.auscape.com.au
THEO ALLOFS / AUSCAPE • www.auscape.com.au
CORBIS AUSTRALIA PTY LTD • www.corbis.com
EMERALD CITY IMAGES • www.emeraldcityimages.com.au
GETTY IMAGES • www.gettyimages.com
JUPITER IMAGES • www.jupiterimages.com.au
ALISON BARNES MARTIN / MASTERFILE • www.masterfile.com
DANIEL J. COX / NATURAL EXPOSURES • www.naturalexposures.com
PETE OXFORD / NATUREPL.COM • www.naturepl.com
PAVEL GERMAN / WILDLIFE IMAGES • www.australiannature.com
PHOTOLIBRARY • www.photolibrary.com
PREMIUM • www.premiumnatur.de
WILDLIGHT PHOTO AGENCY • www.wildlight.net

Detailed page credits for the remarkable photographers whose work appears in *Thank You for Being You*
and other books by Bradley Trevor Greive are freely available at www.btgstudios.com.

When I think about you, I immediately realize
I have a lot to be grateful for. I really do.

I have filed away at least a million things to thank you for,
but somehow I never got around to actually telling you
what I felt nearly as often as I wanted to.

Now, I don't want to appear needy

or crowd you with mushy sentiment.

I just want to look you in the eye and finally say,

"Thank you."

Hang on, that was a bit lame. What I meant to say was,

"THANK YOU!"

Whew, that feels better already. Let me just take a few deep breaths
and center myself. Okay, here we go.

Thank you for all the little things
you have done to make me smile

and basically feel good about myself.

Thank you for the great conversations we've shared
about important issues of global consequence,
and nothing much at all.

Thank you for all the delicious meals we have enjoyed

and for just being good company.

Thank you for all the little things you do to brighten my day—
knowing exactly when to pop in and say hi,

rubbing suntan lotion on my back without getting sand in it,

and showing me how to get around those accursed fish forks.

Thank you for being so thoughtful.
You always seem to put me first.

And I love it that you always remember my birthday
and pretend to forget my age.

I can't tell you how much I appreciate the way
you put up with my nitpicking, whining, and little tantrums, 19

and the fact that I tell my jokes back to front
so there is no punch line. Then I make you wait
while I try to tell it again, and I still get it wrong.

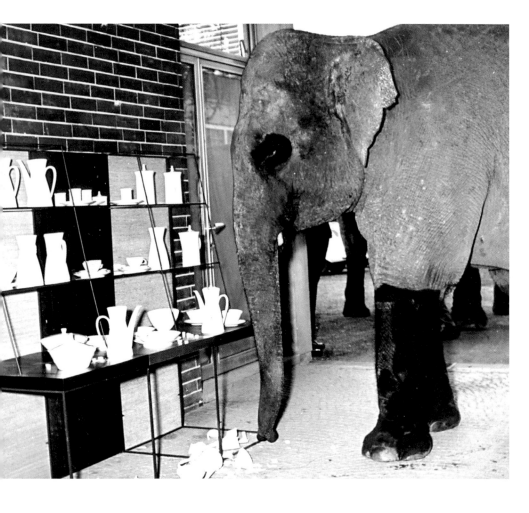

Thank you for ignoring both my general clumsiness
and the awkward moments that follow my little disasters.

Thank you for letting me know when overfed pigeons
are flying overhead.

Thank you for motivating me to get off my butt—

I wouldn't see or do half as much without you.

Thank you for getting me revved up and excited
about all the possibilities life has to offer

and for calming me down when it all gets to be a little too much.

Thank you for making a real effort
when we go out for a night on the town.
I feel fantastic when we are out together having fun.

And no matter how close to death I feel the next morning—
it is always worth it.

Of course, it's not just little things. There are some big things, too, and these are even harder to talk about.

Thank you for finding it in your heart to forgive me
for the things I have done that hurt or upset you.

Thank you for always telling me the truth straight up—
whether it be good news or bad.

Thank you for having the courage and compassion
not to run away screaming when you see me before 8 a.m.

Thank you for going along with my crazy dreams—

and for helping me imagine my name up in lights.

You always make me feel like a superstar.

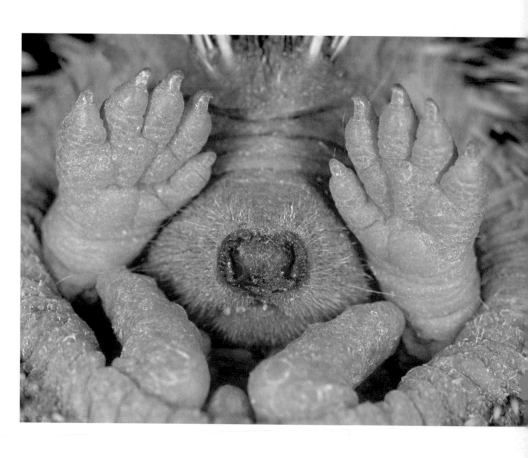

Thank you for helping me come out of my shell,

for showing me there is a life to be had
outside my job and my home,

for helping me see the good things
that are sitting right in front of my nose,

and for teaching me how to laugh and have a great time
no matter where I am.

Thank you for helping me shrug off my emotional baggage

and for not ridiculing my nutty phobias, weird obsessions,
and general craziness.

Thank you for always looking out for me and my best interests

and for encouraging me to eat well, take good care of myself,

keep track of my pennies, and plan for the future.

Thank you for taking my fears seriously.
I am so grateful you are my port in the storm,

dashing to my side in my darkest hour

and helping me take a few baby steps back toward the light.

Thank you for keeping me in your heart and in your prayers,

for your quiet words of encouragement,

and for not letting me walk away without at least
one more compliment than I deserve.

Thank you for being someone
whom I can trust with my most fragile feelings.

Thank you for making me feel safe, comfortable, and happy
whenever I am around you because of all the things you do and,
I suppose, all the things you *never* do.

Thank you for not calling me before noon on Sundays

or anytime during "Must-See TV."

Thank you for not talking over me when we disagree.

And when I don't understand something, I am so grateful
you don't stare at me like I am an idiot

O.R S.P.E.A.K S.L.O.W.L.Y A.N.D L.O.U.D.L.Y
L.I.K.E I A.M A C.O.M.P.L.E.T.E M.O.R.O.N.

Awww, gosh. I know I've forgotten so many amazing things
I wanted to thank you for. Think, think, think!

Oh well. I could never list every wonderful thing you've done anyway, because you've gone out on a limb for me countless times.

Even if I could, mere words of thanks would always be inadequate.
I wish there was a better way to show you how I feel.

In a world full of fakes, you are the real thing. A true friend.

I feel so blessed—of all the billions of people
who could have shared my path, I stumbled across you.

Every kindness you have shown me has touched my heart.

Your generosity has made so many otherwise ordinary days
feel exciting and new.

I treasure every sweet gesture, every little thing you do.
Your friendship is as precious to me as anything on this earth.

Your example has opened up a window into my soul
that lets in the sunshine.

Thanks to your gift of friendship, I can let go of shadows in the past,

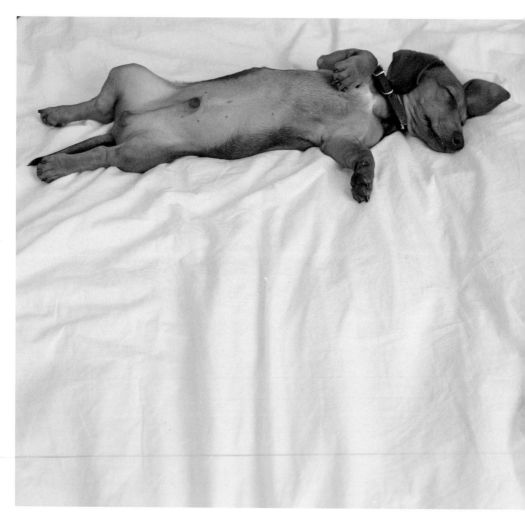

feel happy in my own skin,

and look forward to many bright, happy days ahead.
And so, in closing, I just want to say,

"Thank Youuuuuuuuu!!!"

You're simply the best.

If you have enjoyed this book,
we'd love to hear from you!

Please send your omments to:
Hallmark Books Feedback
P.O. Box 419034
Mail Drop 215
Kansas City, MO 64141

Or e-mail us at:
booknotes@hallmark.com